PEOPLE'S INSTITUTIONS in DECLINE

PEOPLE'S INSTITUTIONS in DECLINE

CAUSES · CONSEQUENCES · CURES

MICHAEL GECAN

Industrial Areas Foundation

PEOPLE'S INSTITUTIONS IN DECLINE
Causes, Consequences, Cures
by Michael Gecan

Edited by Gregory F. Augustine Pierce
Cover and text design and typesetting by Patricia A. Lynch

Published by ACTA Publications, 4848 N. Clark Street, Chicago, IL 60640, (800) 397-2282, www.actapublications.com

Library of Congress Number: 2018932211
ISBN: 978-0-87946-658-9
Printed in the United States of America by Total Printing Systems
Year 30 29 28 27 26 25 24 23 22 21 20 19 18
Printing 10 9 8 7 6 5 4 3 2 First

♻ Text printed on 30% post-consumer recycled paper.

CONTENTS

OVERVIEW

Many voluntary institutions in what Peter Drucker called the "third sector"—families and extended families, congregations, schools, unions, small businesses associations, grassroots and ethnic organizations—are in decline. There is a large and growing set of studies, books, articles, and commentaries about this trend, some of which I've listed in the bibliography. It is a development that observers on almost all points along the political spectrum acknowledge and bemoan. In a country considered hopelessly polarized, on this issue, it seems, there is consensus.

So this essay is not about whether or not these institutions—what I will call "people's institutions" because citizens still control them and the feel some sense of ownership of them—are declining. It is about a second pattern that people across the political spectrum share: the very way we tend to *think and talk about* individuals and institutions has crippled our ability to wrestle with the causes of that decline, to assess the consequences for our communities and our country, and, most importantly, to apply the cures required to make our nation whole and healthy again.

I thought I had a pretty good sense of the price paid by people and places caught in the last half-century of institutional decline. I saw this all first-hand in 1980, when I began my stint as the lead organizer of East Brooklyn Congregations. At that time, East New York was literally the end of the New Lots transit line, but also, with its neighbor Brownsville, it appeared to be the end of the line for a large piece of a modern American city.

A delegation of mayors had toured the area a few

years before. After the tour, Mayor White of Boston, declared: "I have seen the beginning of the end of civilization." While this observation was often made and usually exaggerated, I could see why the mayor responded in that way. In the fall of 1980, as I began to drive and walk the streets of those neighborhoods, I quickly learned that street signs, stop signs, and one-way signs were the exception, not the rule. When I called someone and arranged an appointment, they would direct me by telling me something like "drive six blocks east of Pennsylvania Avenue, turn right at the burned-out factory, then left one block later at the lot filled with tires and construction debris." For a new but seasoned organizer like myself, this was an inconvenience. For someone having a heart attack or a home invaded, however, it could be the difference between life and death. The park and pool in Browns-ville had been under reconstruction for years—leaving kids in that community without their main out-door and sports option. The retail strips were either abandoned or dismal. And at night things got worse. Gun battles were common. One evening, at 9:00 or so, as I headed onto the former Interboro (now Jackie Robinson) Parkway toward my home a few miles into Queens, two groups of gunmen were shooting it out across the parkway. Flashes filled the shrubs on both sides of the road. I did the only thing that occurred to me at the time: I ducked and kept driving.

The official position of the New York City establishment on neighborhoods like East New York and Brownsville and the South Bronx, recorded in the pages of the *New York Times*, was alternately described as "planned shrinkage" or "benign neglect." Both the business community and the political class had reached a consensus: There was no point in throwing any more good money after bad. After a few months, I could see that there was nothing planned about the shrinkage and nothing benign about the neglect. I also began to meet leaders and residents who refused to accept that verdict—made by outsiders with literally no input from the people who lived there. Why didn't they have any say? Because their institutions had already declined to the point where it was too late to fight back.

After nearly four decades organizing in communities like East Brooklyn, I didn't think that I could be surprised by any other analysis or description of American drift and decline. But a few months ago, on March 21, 2017, I was. And the venue for my surprise was as far from the streets of East Brooklyn in 1980 as a person could get—a conference room at the Center Of Theological Inquiry at Princeton. The director of the Center, Will Storrar, had invited me to hear a presentation by Professors Angus Deaton and Anne Case, who both taught at Princeton and happen to be husband and wife. Will is a native of Scotland, as is Angus Deaton, winner of the Nobel Prize for his book, *The Great Escape.*

Will had invited me to other gatherings at the center, but I had declined most of them, confessing my skepticism of most academics and my need to stay focused on my work as a grassroots, institutionally-based organizer. He persisted in his invitations, however, and piqued my interest when he mentioned the work of Deaton and Case. That's how and why and when I got my second big lesson in the decline of people's institutions in the United States.

The morning gathering was attended by about a dozen people—everyone but me an academic, several of whom were from universities in the UK, Germany, and elsewhere. Will opened the session with greetings and mentioned that I was one of several new additions to the group and then introduced the presenters. Anne Case did the bulk of the presentation. She stood at the head of the table and to the left of a large screen. Angus Deaton remained seated nearby and added his insights along the way. Within a few minutes, I realized that all my fears about past academic obfuscation about communities and organization could be set aside—at least for the day.

Anne Case, erect and spare, spoke clearly and directly. And the slides that she showed, combined with her commentary and Deaton's additions, captured the small audience from the start. Their theme was: "Around the turn of the century, after decades of improvement, all-cause mortality rates among white non-Hispanic men and women in middle age stopped falling in the US, and began to rise. While midlife mortality (rates) continued to *fall* in other rich countries, and in other racial and ethnic groups in the US, white non-Hispanic mortality rates for those 45-54 *increased* from 1998 through 2013. Mortality-rate declines from the two biggest killers in middle age—cancer and heart disease—were off-set by marked increases in drug overdoses, suicides, and alcohol-related liver deaths in this period. By 2014, rising mortality (rates) in midlife (for this particular group), led by these 'deaths of despair,' was large enough to offset overall mortality-rate gains for children and the elderly...."

As Anne Case spoke, she used her clicker to bring charts and maps up on the screen. Middle-aged whites, especially white males between 50 and 54, were dying at an increasingly high rate—about 200 per 100,000 higher than black males. [See Figure 1, page 14.] The trend lines showed that somewhere around 2007 white mortality rates equaled and then

Figure 1

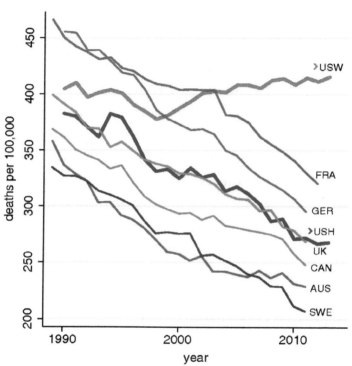

All-cause mortality, ages 45–54 for US White non-Hispanics (USW),
US Hispanics (USH), and six comparison countries: France (FRA),
Germany (GER), the United Kingdom (UK), Canada (CAN),
Australia (AUS), and Sweden (SWE).

From "Rising morbidity and mortality in midlife among white non-
Hispanic Americans in the 21st century," by Anne Case and Angus
Deaton

exceeded black mortality. Another slide showed that drug, alcohol, and suicide mortality rates for all whites in that same age bracket was at least twice the rate of people in Australia, Canada, Germany, France, and Sweden. [See Figure 1, page 14.] A set of maps showed how the increase in mortality rates in the non-Hispanic white population has spread across the US, with deep concentrations of early deaths in the mid-south, south, southwest, rural California and Oregon, and even parts of Maine and New England. Mortality rates for this population started to rise in the US and fall in Europe in the year 2000, and the deadliest places in the nation by 2017, Deaton and Case said, were the southwest corner of West Virginia, the southeast corner of Kentucky, and Baltimore—the city where so many working-class whites from West Virginia have migrated.

Case and Deaton didn't need to add any rhetorical flourishes or high-tech visual gimmicks to their presentation. They kept their remarks and their slides simple and spare—and all the more powerful, I thought, because of that. And they discussed the factors that could have contributed to these trends—the loss of jobs, the influx of opioids and other drugs, the breakdown of family life, and other factors. They were clearly concerned by what they had found and what they were presenting. But, as professionals, they were presenting the facts as they saw them. It was quiet and clinical. It was an autopsy.

When they concluded, Will Storrar led a serious discussion of the group's reactions to the presentation. I was struck by the graphs and maps. My comment was that I believed that there was another set of graphs "behind" the trend-lines that had been shown that morning. My guess was that this other set of graphs would show how some key institutions—unions, churches, civic groups, local businesses—had declined both as a precondition for this epidemic of death and ill health and as a contributing cause. I thought of how East Brooklyn had looked and felt in the early 1980's—isolated, neglected, stripped of street signs and one-way signs and most indicators of normal healthy communal life, literally and figuratively off the map.

Those dark stretches of mortality-rate increases on the maps Case and Deaton presented—in rural and exurban counties in Kentucky and Ohio and West Virginia and western Oregon and scores of other places, expanding year by year—were mini-versions of what I had observed in East Brooklyn in 1980. The difference now was that the people dying in record numbers were not primarily poor and blue-collar African Americans and Hispanics, but mostly poor and blue-collar whites.

When had all this new discrepancy in mortality rates among people of different ethnic and racial backgrounds started? The usual response is that the deterioration of the quality of life for African Americans and Hispanics, particularly in our inner cities, had begun in the 1960s and was now slowing down or even reversing, while the decline for non-Hispanic whites began much later, perhaps in the late 1980s or even the 1990s. But I'm not so sure.

I recalled a morning in 1965. It was February 1, a Monday, and my family and I woke up to front page news about two guys I knew well. We lived on the corner of Springfield and Ferdinand in the West Garfield Park neighborhood of Chicago. At the time, it was tough, blue-collar, and white. Across the street, a few years before, the Del Vecchio family had bought a home—444 North Springfield. The family was unique in one way. The mother was a single parent, divorced or separated from her husband. George Del Vecchio was about my age at the time—16. When he moved into the area, he decided that he would establish himself as the toughest guy around. He needed to prove himself against the person who held that title at the time—Mike Stepkowicz. He waited in a gangway one afternoon for Stepkowicz to walk by. Then he walked out, cold-cocked him, and beat him half to death. From then on, George was the one who called the shots. One of his closest friends was another tough fellow—Joey Varchetto. Varchetto was the center fielder on our baseball team. We played our league games at Kells Field on Chicago Avenue and

Homan. In the middle of the last season, as we struggled as a .500 team, Joey called a players-only meeting. He said: "No more losing. The next guy makes us lose, I'm going to kill." We never doubted that Joey meant this literally. My teammates and I played as if our lives depended on it. We went undefeated the rest of the way.

Both George and Joey were already using drugs—barbiturates, also called "goof balls" or "pep pills." George also had a rifle, which he showed off to us one afternoon in his basement. He also pulled a sheet from a closet, smeared with blood. "My father's blood," he said. "Wish I'd killed the bastard." We didn't know if the story was true, but not one of us thought to challenge him.

One Sunday night, George and Joey and a third guy, Eugene Waswill, got high and went out to find more money for more pills with a handgun we didn't know they had. They spotted a man, Fred A. Christiansen, taking a walk near his home a few miles north of our neighborhood. They shot him, but Christiansen, wounded, cried for help. Then Del Vecchio fired five more bullets into him, killing him for the $11 they found in his wallet. Because Del Vecchio and Varchetto were just sixteen, they were tried as juveniles. They served time and were released at age twenty-one. Del Vecchio killed again—this time the six-year-old son of his girlfriend—and was executed by the State of Illinois. Varchetto was gunned down by a rival gangster some years later. I don't know what happened to Waswill.

So already, in 1965, I experienced personally one stark chapter in what would unfold over time as the story of urban decline: guns, gangs, drugs, family breakdown, and violent deaths. And in the next year or so, the second chapter would unfold. It featured the massive double exodus: the first of African American families out of slum conditions and into white working-class blocks; the second the frightened flight of those white families into nearby neighborhoods or expanding suburbs. I was right in the middle of that in Chicago.

Two summers after the Christiansen murder, my family began getting calls from real estate brokers. They phoned incessantly, deep in the night at times, sometimes in the middle of the night, with this message: "The blacks are coming; your house is losing value every day; move now or lose everything, or stay and get knifed by one of them." These unscrupulous "realtors" spoke whatever language the person at the other end of the line spoke—a Croatian broker calling those of us who were Croatians, an Italian calling Italians, a Pole calling Poles. The sound of that summer was of deep rumble and shifting gears of moving trucks. Day after day, trucks rolled down Springfield, Avers, Harding and across Ferdinand, Ohio, Huron, taking the belongings of our neighbors out and delivering the furniture of our new black neighbors in. Some of our neighbors, embarrassed to be seen fleeing, literally had the truck come in the middle of the night.

By the end of the summer, the section of our parish area, Our Lady of the Angels, that had been 99.5% white (one black family had lived in isolation but relative peace at the end of our block) was now 99.5%

black (my family remained only because my Croatian immigrant grandmother, not five-foot-tall but tough as nails, refused to leave). The terms for this money-making scheme—"panic peddling" or "block busting"—were familiar to every on-the-edge blue collar ethnic family in any big city in the US. This drama had victims and villains and rhythms. For some, the victims were the hardworking white families that felt threatened and forced to run, losing whatever equity they had built up in their homes, severing life-long relationships, re-starting in another neighborhood. And the villains, to us, were the black families that brought crime and decay with them, like so many extra pieces of luggage. But as I learned not that much later in my life, the victims were also the black families who were desperate to get out of rat infested apartments in the ghetto, eager to own a home of their own and see their kids play in a fenced backyard and attend a decent school. And they were victimized by those who left and refused to welcome them into our neighborhoods and churches and schools.

The real villains, of course, were the well-organized team of real estate operators, landlords, mortgage brokers, and local machine politicians (who cried crocodile tears as neighborhood after neighborhood was destroyed and re-segregated while they raked in cash and favors from the crowd that drove and profited from the process).

This housing dynamic distilled the relentless erosion of one of the prime foundations of working class life—an affordable home, slowly gaining equity, in a stable neighborhood—into a racial psychodrama of black versus white and white versus black. And it masked another pattern of slow and undramatic unraveling that had already begun to weaken neighborhoods like the one I lived in as a kid.

I asked a data scientist based in the Twin Cities, David Kamper, to help me look further at the causes and consequences of the unraveling of people's institutions. He went to work and produced several graphs produced here that I believe help explain the conditions underlying the analysis Professors Case and Deaton described on that March day in Princeton.

Consider the state of unions. The percent of wage and salary workers who were union members peaked in 1955 or so, at 33%. [See Figure 2, page 25.] By 1965 union membership had dipped considerably, to 28%. More than one in seven union jobs had already disappeared. That steady loss continued—dropping to its current rate of about 12%. In Chicago, union membership was still prized. My father couldn't break into the construction trades as a plasterer, so eventually gave it up and ran a tavern and worked as a security guard. The main trade unions were adjuncts of the Chicago Cook County Democratic Machine, just as modern service unions are often extensions of today's Democratic Party around the country. That meant that union workers benefited from favorable wage and benefits levels controlled by the Machine (and its partners in the real estate and finance sectors). But it also meant that union members had to put up with block busting and panic peddling. If the

Figure 2

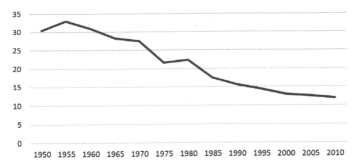

Percent of wage and salary workers who are members of unions

Gerald Mayer, "Union Membership Trends in the United States," Congressional Research Service, Bureau of Labor Statistics Current Population Survey Data

Machine said move, you had to move, usually to a neighborhood farther from your workplace and maybe even out of the city itself. And that meant, for millions of Americans, that they could no longer walk to work, which 10% could do in 1960 and under 4% could do by 1990. The increased hourly wages made by a union worker, therefore, was often lost when homes lost value and block-busting realtors pushed families further west or north or south. My parents moved twice, losing financial ground each time, like hundreds of thousands of others. They sold to African American families being gouged by real estate brokers and also losing financial ground each time. But the larger point is that even in the 1950s and 1960s, unions in Chicago and the country were already ten years into their now sixty-five-year decline. Even where they were still considered "strong," the unions had made deals with the urban political machines whose cynical strategies added steep hidden costs to the very union members who were supporting them.

Roman Catholic churches are another people's institution that is in rapid decline today, much like

Figure 3

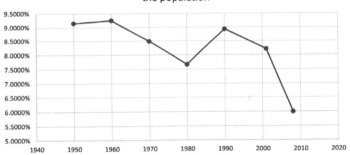

Methodists, Presbyterians and Episcopals as a percentage of the population

Historical Statistics of the United States, Colonial Times to 1970, US Census Bureau, American Religious Identification Survey, US Census Bureau

US Religion Census, Association of Statisticians of American Religious Bodies

their Protestant brethren experienced decades ago. The Catholic churches remained fairly stable across these decades, but this is a more complicated story than simply a tale of overall membership. In effect, white ethnic Roman Catholics moved, or were driven, from the cities into the first and then outer rings of suburbs. They left their former neighborhoods and parishes with weaker finances, poorer parishioners, and closing schools. Only the influx of Hispanic Roman Catholics has so far saved the denomination from the same fate as mainline Protestant groups.

Protestant denominations followed the same pattern as unions. Membership in Methodist, Presbyterian, and Episcopal denominations peaked in the mid-1950's [see Figure 3, page 27] at around 9 % of the entire population. By 1980 it was 7.5%. And currently it is under 6%.

Here's another institution that declined. The percentage of the US population in psychiatric facilities hit a high of 0.33% in 1950, declined to a little over 0.20% in 1965, and is now almost negligible—.02 % [see Figure 4, page 29]. This might seem like an odd

Figure 4

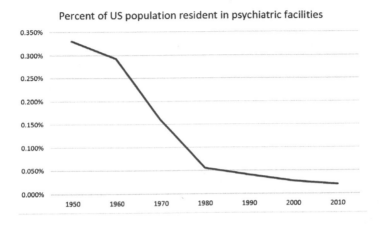

Percent of US population resident in psychiatric facilities

National Association of State Mental Health Program Directors (NASMHD)

institution for me to include in this list. There were certainly reasons for doubting the quality and efficacy of mental asylums. Many were dreadfully run—little more than holding pens for the mentally ill. And yet for the approximately 4% of those with serious mental illness in the country, they represented at least a partial solution.

The response to the well documented abuses and limitations of what we call "mental institutions" was not to improve them; it was to dismantle them and promise to create an alternative system of community mental health facilities and treatment options. That alternative system was never built. The people pushed out of asylums ended up in two places— homeless on the streets of every city and town in America, or prisoners in a cell. The explosion of jail and prison facilities, where experts now estimate that up to 30% of the inmates are mentally ill, was in large part a by-product of the loss of institutional psychiatric facilities. In 1965, the percentage of people in US prisons was at its lowest, at 0.1% of the total population of the US. In 1980 the trend line has tipped

Figure 5

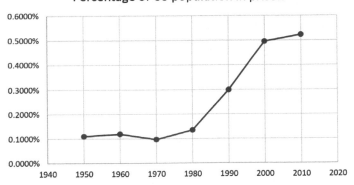

Percentage of US population in prison

US Bureau of Justice Statistics

upward—way upward. [See Figure 5, page 31.] By 2010 the number of mentally ill in jail or prison was five times higher than it was fifteen years before. We don't even know what that figure is today.

George Del Vecchio's mother, terrified by her son's temper and tantrums, saw trouble coming and had tried to find him a psychiatric treatment facility. But she couldn't bring herself to put him in a youth home that had earned its poor reputation, and she simply decided to hope and pray that he "would grow out of his condition."

While we could see and hear the moving trucks, observe the handguns and avoid the gunfire, swallow or flee the pills and other drugs displayed by pushers, track the blocks shifting from all-white to all-black in the course of a single summer, we at least had institutions, however flawed, that were "ours" that we could turn to or not turn to back when I was young. But the history of the slow and steady erosion of one set of institutions and the slow and steady growth of another set of very different institutions was largely hidden or ignored or denied.

But why do we not really understand these trends? In part, that is because, instead of thinking institutionally, most of us think individually. In fact the very word—"institutional"—has now almost an entirely negative connotation. And the process of "de-institutionalizing" an organization or a process is almost always assumed to be a wonderful thing. Hugh Heclo, who wrote a fine book about this topic, *On Thinking Institutionally*, put it this way: "Institutional thinking seems to be one of the main things missing when all sorts of events repeatedly befoul American public life, involving both individuals and organizations. Its absence is a much-felt presence, but we do not seem to have a way of discussing it."

In this essay, I'm trying to find a way of discussing the challenges to people's institutions. Let me start with a set of examples.

If we think individually about young men and guns and violence, we focus on the pathological personality of individuals like George Del Vecchio and Joey Varchetto—who were front page news for days in the Chicago papers in 1965. Fifty years later, Chicago is awash in murder and mayhem; and the average murder barely makes it into what's left of the two daily papers, which dutifully report the weekly casualty count. The fact that the Memorial Day weekend this year was marred by "only" fifty-two shootings—including seven homicides—was considered progress. That number was about twenty fewer than the Memorial Day bloodbath of a year earlier. A few months later, over the Fourth of July holiday, the trend reversed again. There were 102 shootings, including fifteen homicides, over that blood-soaked weekend.

We tend to think individually about this dynamic—about the actions of individual young men, now black and Hispanic and jobless for the most part. The responses are individually oriented too. One set of responses involves tracking, arresting, and jailing every single bad guy in the neighborhood. In essence, that's been the dominant response. Cook County Jail is filled to its limit with some 10,000 prisoners. Other state and county facilities are also crowded. The decades of wholesale arrest and incarceration have had little impact on the rate of violence. In fact, there is some evidence that breaking up the one institution that many of these young men affiliated with—i.e., local gangs—led to an increase in more random and less organized violence by more decentralized and detached criminals. On the more therapeutic end of the response spectrum, the latest theory is that each individual needs activities and programs—such as basketball leagues. Each individual needs job training—although people seem to ignore the fact that there are no jobs once the training ends. Each individual needs a mentor. Each individual needs a GED or a way into community college. Each individual family needs a housing voucher so it can shop around from one desperate ghetto to the next for a slightly less rat-infested apartment or home. The concept is to try to improve each individual, one by one, person by person, need by need, so that, someday, somehow, conditions will begin to change.

If we are thinking individually about all those Americans between 45 and 54 dying in America right now and the broader group of ninety-one individuals each day losing their lives to opioids and heroin, we think about lost souls, desperate individuals, who have succumbed one by one to the incredible power of these drugs. But if we are thinking institutionally, as Sam Quinones forces the readers of his book, *Dreamland*, to do, we see how the spread of opioids was systematically organized by the pharmaceutical industry, how that industry used flimsy research to declare opioids non-addictive and then sent scores of thousands of salespeople out to saturate doctors' offices and medical facilities and drug stores with those pills. And we learn how network of gangsters in one area of Mexico sent thousands of young men north to the Midwest and other non-inner-city parts of the country to peddle the black tar heroin that became the needed next high for those who could no longer be satisfied by opioids. If we are thinking institutionally, we can clearly see how this tragedy unfolded, scene by scene, community by community.

There is little or no consideration given to the state of the institutions that have decayed in these communities—decent housing complexes that once had tenants councils and community clean ups, athletic leagues that were led and coached by neighborhood parents, public spaces, like the swimming pool Quinones features in Dreamland, where people met and related and held one another accountable, religious institutions where people felt supported enough to share their family struggles, local schools that drew from the blocks around them, and, yes, bowling leagues studied by writer Robert Putnam that attracted entire families on a Friday night. Thinking institutionally means thinking about whether it is possible to begin to rebuild these—or other and more relevant—institutions in sections of these communities.

Thinking individually has shaped how we interpret our own social and political history. When we are thinking individually about someone like Rosa Parks, we accept the myth that she was a singular and courageous woman who finally decided, on her own, that she just couldn't take the humiliation of sitting in the back of the bus and decided to sit wherever she wanted.

If we are thinking institutionally, we recognize that Rosa Parks was courageous, but not singular and spontaneous. She had trained at the Highlander Center in Tennessee to be a civil rights leader. She had tried her tactic of sitting in a forbidden section of the bus several times before, unsuccessfully. She had, in fact, rehearsed her action before attracting the media attention that she desired.

When we think individually about someone like Mayor Rahm Emanuel, we accept the notion that he is a more modern Democrat, more independent, more progressive, more modern than his predecessors on the fifth floor of City Hall. But if we are thinking institutionally, we realize that one of Emanuel's first jobs, as a very young man, was fundraising for then-States Attorney and future mayor Richard M. Daley. We would know that he ran for Congress because the Cook County Democratic Machine was worried about the popularity of a candidate who truly was more progressive and independent of the Machine. Emanuel was made to appear to be independent and won the primary.

We would also recall that in his one private sector excursion, Emanuel worked for Wasserstein Perella. During that two-year stint, Emanuel made $16 million. Once Barack Obama won the presidency, he tapped Emanuel to be his first chief of staff (followed a few years later by William M. Daley). In other words, if we are thinking institutionally, we would understand that Rahm Emanuel is as much a product of the Machine as Richard M. Daley, William Daley...or Barack Obama himself.

When we think individually about the former president, we see him as a gifted writer, eloquent speaker, and unique figure. He was—and still is—a gifted writer and skillful figure. And what he embodied and represented—the first African American to be elected president—was unique and remarkable. We can appreciate and acknowledge all of these aspects of his life.

If we think about him institutionally, however, we see him as a part of the Cook County Democratic Machine as well. After he lost his first race for Congress, he made his peace with the Machine and won an Illinois State Senate seat. The leader of the senate, Emil Jones Sr., was at the time a veteran south side Machine operative, just as the speaker of the Assembly, Michael Madigan Jr., was and still is a second-generation southwest side powerhouse. Then-state-senator Obama was part of a generation of ambitious political figures that included Rahm Emanuel, Lisa Madigan (daughter of Michael Madigan Jr.), Rod Blagojevich (who had married higher up into the Machine by taking Patty Mell, daughter of a north side Polish Machine leader, Ed Mell, as his wife), and former journalist and then political consultant David Axelrod. Emil Jones Sr. referred to the young Barack Obama as his "son" (in addition to his son by blood, Emil Jones Jr.). And Barack referred to Emil Jones Sr. as his "father." When Obama wanted to run for the US Senate, he needed only one vote—Emil Jones Sr.'s vote, the Machine's vote, to ensure that he would have a very good chance to win. Win he did.

If we continue to think institutionally about Obama, we can see that the new president made a fateful decision: instead of using his presidency to break free of the Chicago machine culture, at least in part, he brought that culture with him into the White House—Rahm Emanuel, David Axelrod, Bill Daley, Valerie Jarrett (daughter of the African American newspaper empire in Chicago), and Penny Pritzker (of the Hyatt Hotel family that funded and supported Machine mayors loyally and was rewarded in turn).

Now, if we are thinking individually about the current president, Donald Trump we might see him as drain-the-swamp champion of all those who think Washington and its elites have betrayed the rest of the nation. Or we can view him as a disconnected, erratic, dangerous individual subject to no influence or constraint.

But if we are thinking institutionally, we take into account that Trump was a product of a father who was a major real estate operator in New York. He grew up in a household and in a culture packed with ambitious, often vain, strongly ego-driven people and organizations that vied with one another to build the tallest and most impressive buildings in a city full of such structures. We appreciate that this world was cut-throat and relentless—with each self-made brand competing with the other brands. In that world, Donald Trump was never the top dog. He was at best tied for fourth, behind bigger builders like Stephen Ross, of the Related Companies, who wasn't satisfied with totally transforming the west side of Manhattan with his multi-billion-dollar Hudson Yards development but had to buy the Miami Dolphins football team as well. We would understand that one of Trump's daughters married the scion of another metropolitan New York real estate empire—the Kushner family of New Jersey. If we are thinking institutionally, we see that Trump has brought the patterns and habits of a lifetime (two lifetimes, if you include his father) in real estate and deal making into the White House. And you see that he's decided to rely on two other institutions to fill out his new administration. One—Wall Street, equal or greater than the real estate industry in the power structure of New York—is represented by people like former Goldman Sachs bigwigs Mnuchin and Cohn. The other, somewhat surprising, was the US military, where he found General Mattis and General McMaster, among others.

Thinking institutionally is not the same as thinking "about" institutions, as Hugh Heclo warns. It is not thinking critically from a lofty academic or ideological distance. It is thinking from inside of institutions and out from there. Thinking institutionally does not diminish the courage of Rosa Parks in any way. Her courage had to be summoned repeatedly as she failed in her first few tries to dramatize the injustice of being treated as a second-class citizen. But it does give us an insight into how most social change happens—that it is planned, organized, rehearsed, refined, until it hits its target and makes its impact.

Thinking institutionally about Rahm Emanuel does not mean we dismiss him or operate out of a stance of cynicism. It just means that we are clear about who he is politically and who he is not. It means that we don't project a superficial image of a modern independent type of new Democrat on him; we see clearly that we are dealing with an elected official with relationships, obligations, and interests that are intimately tied to the Democratic Machine.

Thinking institutionally about Barack Obama does not lessen the extraordinary and stunning fact of his election and what that election represented to African Americans and many other Americans. But it does help us understand how his administration could give the nation's banks a pass during the dreadful foreclosure crisis of 2009 and 2010 and consign up to five million American homeowners to years of housing loss, underwater mortgages, and acute financial stress. This was a replay, fifty years later, of the way the Chicago machine sided with the real estate and banking industries against the interests of the very blue-collar homeowners who supported it loyally in every election.

And thinking institutionally about Donald Trump does not exonerate him from the damage he is trying to do—if you happen to be an opponent of the new president—or minimize the remarkable fact that he outmaneuvered the entire Republican establishment in the primary and the entire Democratic establishment in the general election to become president. But it does provide a perspective as to why he operates as he does, who he relies on (yes, it's not just him, alone, with his Twitter account, on the second floor of the White House each night) for advice and to carry out his policies, and what levers could be pulled to counter his actions in the future.

1

Why do we think individually
and not institutionally?

THE PREFERENCE FOR
"FREEDOM FROM"

Why is it that most of the time we think individually and not institutionally? I can think if six reasons—which overlap and reinforce one another.

The first is that we are fundamentally a "freedom from" country. Freedom from—or negative freedom—was hard wired into the political founding of our republic. "The Bill of Rights," wrote historian James McPherson, "is an excellent example of negative liberty. Nearly all of the first ten amendments to the Constitution apply the phrase 'shall not' to the federal government. In fact, eleven of the first twelve amendments placed limitations on the power of the national government." The basic posture of the citizens of this new republic was *defensive*. At times, they needed to rally, grudgingly and haltingly, after other options had been tried, to defend that limited government against other, worse forms of government. But once free of the crown or clerics or other forms of tyranny, they proved to be just as wary of their own newly but minimally formed government.

Thomas Jefferson was also wary of another set of

institutions—commercial monopolies. In 1787, after the Constitution had been drafted, Jefferson wrote Madison, "I will now tell you what I do not like. First, the omission of a bill of rights, providing clearly, and without the aid of sophism, for freedom of religion, freedom of the press, protection against standing armies, restriction of monopolies, the eternal and unremitting force of the habeas corpus laws, and trials by jury...." A year later, after Madison drafted the Bill of Rights and it was heading toward ratification, Jefferson wrote again, "By a declaration of rights, I mean one which shall stipulate freedom of religion, freedom of the press, freedom of commerce against monopolies, trial by juries in all cases, no suspension of the habeas corpus, no standing armies. These are fetters against doing evil, which no honest government should decline." Jefferson had studied the evil done by the British East India Company and saw the damage that monopolies could do. But he lost that argument. And our founding documents said nothing about the potentially coercive and abusive powers of monopolies and much about the potentially coercive and abusive powers of government itself.

"The doctrine that accumulations of power can never be too great," the great philosopher Isaiah Berlin wrote, "provided that they are rationally controlled and used, ignores the central reason for pursuing liberty in the first place—that all paternalistic government, however benevolent, cautious, disinterested, and rational, have tended, in the end, to treat the majority of men as minors, or as being too often incurably foolish or irresponsible; or else as maturing so slowly as not to justify their liberation at any clearly foreseeable date (which, in practice, means at no definite time at all). This is a policy which degrades men, and seems to me to rest on no rational or scientific foundation, but, on the contrary, on a profoundly mistaken view of the deepest human needs."

The American experiment was emerging out of several hundred years of catastrophic war, colonization, and repression. Final solutions proposed and enforced primarily by governments dominated by monarchs and clerics had decimated both the old and new worlds. *Freedom from*—not an expression of soaring rhetoric or wild aspiration—was, at the time, a logical and rarely reached goal. Profound distrust of all concentrations of governmental power, even the power of our own new government, became part of our national DNA. That distrust was dramatically reinforced—and profoundly deepened—by the murderous rise of Communism and Fascism in the 1930s and 1940s. But distrust of the equally dangerous concentrated power of commercial monopolies, most evident on the other side of the world, worried Jefferson but not many others and has only intermittently emerged as a major theme in American history.

2

Why do we think individually
and not institutionally?

MAGICAL THINKING
ABOUT THE MARKET

The second reason for our tendency to think individually rather than institutionally is an outgrowth of the first—the increasingly central and dominant role of the market sector. In organizing, we say that a healthy society is one where there is an inter-play of three distinct sectors—the market, the government, and what the late great Peter Drucker called the third sector, or civil society, where voluntary institutions like congregations and civic associations thrive. At times, those sectors cooperate. At times, those sectors are in conflict. We must take Isaiah Berlin's warning about the inevitable drift of government toward paternalism and apply it to the market and to the civic sectors as well. *Any entity*—business, church, governmental, political party, community—that accumulates too much power, that dominates its own sector and the other two sectors, will end up treating the majority of men and women as minors and will degrade them in the long run. Dominant power, unilateral power, unaccountable power in any sector's hands will trend toward total power—otherwise, known as totalitarianism.

The market, with increasing success, has made a claim for immunity from this universal tendency to accumulate power. In part, big business pretends not even to be an institution or a sector. It poses as a pure and uncontrolled dynamic, free of the bloated bureaucracies and rules of the governmental sector, more nimble and responsive than the slow and relational scale and scope of civic and community life. As a dynamic, it neither wants nor needs nor tolerates buffers or barriers or mediating institutions—such as governmental regulators setting limits or civic groups demanding environmental clean-ups—between it and its individual consumers and communities. These buffers and barriers are considered unnecessary restraints on what is supposed to be the invisible and almost mystical workings of the market.

Adam Smith, who mentioned "the invisible hand" first in 1759 and only two other times in his entire career, never mentioned "the market" or "capitalism" as we now know them. He was reflecting on the productivity of small manufacturers and farmers. But as time went on, as the modern market and modern capitalism grew in power, their promoters married the belief in the wisdom of an invisible hand to a second article of faith—Schumpeter's notion of "creative destruction." The invisible hand of the market knew instinctively what to destroy and what to spare. No one could be blamed when whatever act of destruction or preservation happened to occur. From this article of faith, it was concluded that the worst thing that could happen would be for government or the civic sector to meddle with this magical process.

Whole schools of economists—from Frankfurt to the University of Chicago to Stanford, and almost every place in between—have promoted these articles of faith. Occasionally a thoughtful economist like Wolfgang Streeck in his book, *Buying Time*, challenges this orthodoxy. "Contrary to what economic theory and ideology would have us believe, capitalism is not a state of nature but a historical social order in need of institutionalization and legitimation; its concrete forms change with time and place and are in principle both susceptible to renegotiation and in danger of breaking down."

3

Why do we think individually
and not institutionally?

THE IDEOLOGY
AND BILLIONS
OF MODERN LIBERTARIANS

The economists' notions of the invisible hand and the inevitability and necessity of creative destruction have also been applauded and supported by a loose group of extraordinarily wealthy libertarian ideologues—a virtual Greek chorus of self-made billionaires. And their work and influence comprise the third reason why we all find it harder and harder to think institutionally instead of individually.

Of the ten wealthiest men in America—Bill Gates, Jeff Bezos, Warren Buffett, Mark Zuckerberg, Larry Ellison, Michael Bloomberg, Charles Koch, David Koch, Larry Page, and Sergey Brin—at least six by my count are libertarians. The Koch brothers are obvious. By so are the founders of Google—Page and Brin—and the founder of Amazon, Bezos. Zuckerberg is a baby-faced and more complex figure—somewhat like basketball whiz Steph Curry—but until recently the founder of Facebook has been a product of the libertarian camp.

Another billionaire, who did not make this list, Peter Thiel, an early funder of Zuckerberg and founder of PayPal and other platforms, described the mission of modern libertarianism this way in his manifesto on the Cato Institute's website: "In our time, the great task for libertarians is to find an escape from politics in all its forms—from the totalitarian and fundamentalist catastrophes to the unthinking demos that guides so-called 'social democracy....' We are in a deadly race between politics and ideology.... The fate of the world may depend on the effort of single person who builds or propagates the machinery of freedom that makes the world safe for capitalism."

It has been a long time since Margaret Thatcher uttered her famous quote, "There is no such thing as society. There are only individual men and women and their families." In Thatcher's case, the head of a government was making the case not to improve, streamline, and reorganize the agencies and departments of the public sector but to dismantle them entirely and sell them off, piece by piece, to the private sector. She was putting into practice what a political philosopher called the libertarian's belief in "the non-reality of other institutions." Ronald Reagan said it in a slightly different way, simply asserting that government wasn't the solution to America's problems; government was the problem. Thatcher proved to be made of sterner stuff. She took her rhetoric and applied it to the agencies and the unions of the government she headed. Reagan seemed satisfied with the rhetoric and, with a few exceptions, downsized very little.

Thirty years later, the enemy of American progress and prosperity has been redefined. In the manifesto of Peter Thiel and the machinations of those like him, the enemy isn't just government; it is the "unthinking demos;" it is the entirety of modern democratic political life; it is every form of freedom except those sanctioned and dispensed by a very small cadre of market and technology true believers. The voting and participating public, unpredictable and amorphous, must be pushed aside. The supposedly objective and quantifiable metrics of the market—its level of confidence in the status of the state—are what count today.

4

Why do we think individually
and not institutionally?

THE USE OF SOCIAL MEDIA
AS A GLOBAL BULLHORN
AND BULLETIN BOARD

The market and its libertarian leaders and thinkers have an enormously powerful tool at their disposal, a tool that they in many cases designed or capitalized at critical points—the Internet and the social media platforms that dominate it. Here's how British writer Alan Finlayson described the dynamic in the UK during and after the recent Brexit vote in a recent piece in the *London Review of Books*: "Newer, better, and rapidly expanding means of creating, harvesting, and analyzing data about human beings' behavior and choices were now available. Hence the second reason the post-bureaucrats didn't believe in old-fashioned democracy. You don't need clumsy things like parties, trade unions, and newspapers if information about what people think, want, feel, and expect is available continuously and in real time from every click and keystroke, online purchase, and below-the-line comment. This is a politics that doesn't prize knowledge of society ("there is no such thing"). It values the generation and interpretation of facts about individuals' behavior and interactions— what they signify or might herald, how to manage and manipulate them. In this world, people do not need to know and understand things about themselves; they are the things to be known about...."

The myth of the liberating and potent possibilities of social media is almost as popular as the myth of the brilliant invisible hand of the market. When the Arab Spring started in Egypt, the established media focused on the use of social media as a tool of those rising up against an oppressive state. I was skeptical and asked three of our young Muslim organizers—one Syrian, one Pakistani, and one Egyptian, if they wanted to spend three weeks in Cairo and listen to the accounts of the people who were leading the actions there. They were eager to go and learned something that almost never made it into the accounts of the unrest: the groups and organizations involved in the actions had been working for years in a very old-fashioned way: taxi drivers talking to taxi drivers, leaders in mosques and Islamic Centers beginning to get to know and build trust with one another, leaders from unions meeting with leaders from religious and civic institutions. In other words, the unrest and the actions that the world viewed each night were the product of relationships and strategies that had been brewing for at least a decade. Social media technology was useful as a kind of bulletin board, but not much more. And, as has been seen since, the opponents of the democratic movement in the country quickly countered by using social media to spread false rumors about respected leaders, to announce actions and gatherings that were not real (attracting people, who went away disappointed and upset at the perceived incompetence of the leadership), and to promote fronts for the next phase of repression in the country. We no longer need to cite Egypt as an example of this threat. Russian operatives used social media to intervene in the 2016 presidential election right here at home.

I'm not claiming that the decline of people's institutions is coordinated in any way. It's not a plot, not a conspiracy. It's something more powerful. It's a synergy—"a mutually advantageous conjunction or compatibility," as the Merriam-Webster Dictionary defines it.

A nation that has a fundamental tendency toward *freedom from* and was forged in reaction to corrupt and repressive institutions famously failed to deal with two threats to its existence—slavery and monopoly. The butcher's bill for the avoidance of the slavery issue was more than 600,000 dead on the battlefields and in the hospitals of the Civil War and many more thousands lynched, shot, beaten to death, and blown up as they sat in their churches. The cost of monopoly—in poisoned workers, polluted rivers and lakes and cities, lead-damaged children, unemployed who die deaths of despair through alcohol or drugs or suicide—might well be as high; and it is still climbing. Our nation struggled, at times, with whether and how to hold the market accountable, most dramatically under two presidents named Roosevelt. Teddy Roosevelt broke up the big trusts and dramatically expanded the nation's national parks—an enormous expansion of the public sector to the dismay of those who saw coal and copper and gold in those mountains and plains. Franklin Delano Roosevelt created an entire infrastructure of public institutions and agencies that enabled workers to organize and provided individuals and families with a full menu of social-insurance options. The very nature of social insurance was created to protect people against the vagaries and pressures of the market. As A. J. Baime wrote about FDR in *The Arsenal of Democracy*, "The New Deal had inserted government into big business as never before. 'They are unanimous in their hate for me,' he said of Wall Street and industrial tycoons in a campaign speech for his second term in 1936. 'And I welcome their hatred.'"

For every action that sought to energize the public sector and reinforce the third or civic sector, there was a reaction. Libertarians worked hard to harmonize the theme of *freedom from*—like the beat of a bass that threads through a piece of music—with the rhythms of an unencumbered market; and they used the social media platforms that they invented and monopolized to project that harmony relentlessly and globally.

The first four trends that I've cited here—the preference for *freedom from*, magical thinking about the market, the ideology and billions of modern libertarians, and the use of social media as a global bullhorn and bulletin board—have evolved and intersected in fits and starts since the New Deal. They have never been in greater harmony. And the addition of two other factors makes them an extraordinarily formidable force in our time.

···•>> 5 <<•···

Why do we think individually and not institutionally?

OUR CULTURE'S OBSESSION WITH THE INDIVIDUAL AND INDIVIDUAL RIGHTS

The fifth trend making us think more individually than institutionally is our culture's obsession with the individual and individual rights. William Sullivan writes, "The basic notions of liberal philosophy far antedate the seventeenth century, but it was the English thinkers of that period, Thomas Hobbes and John Locke, who gave the new system of ideas a structure which has remained essentially intact ever since.... The primary human reality is the individual, conceived independently of social relationships.... The only ultimate source of value in society is individual preference and will.... The effect was to dissolve values into power, specifically, power to augment and foster the individual's passion-driven will.... With this vision goes a correlative notion of knowledge as the reduction of complex wholes to simple elements. In this, liberalism is closely tied to the modern scientific view of knowledge as the power to analyze and recombine elements for the sake of control."

Before I give some practical examples of this obsession with individual rights, let me say that I was first exposed to the possibilities of organizing at the age of sixteen by being taken by my high school Jesuit instructors at St. Ignatius in Chicago to actions and meetings of the struggling Civil *Rights* Movement. The dignity and courage of the leaders that I saw risking their lives in open housing marches on the southwest side and other neighborhoods remain vivid and inspiring to this day, more than a half-century later. I participated, in a small way, as a young organizer in the anti-apartheid movement. Bishop Desmond Tutu, through Trinity Church Wall Street in New York City, sent clergy and community leaders to the US for rest and recuperation, all during the last decade of the apartheid era. And, once Nelson Mandela was released, my colleague Arnie Graf and I (along with my wife Sheila and then young children, Joe, Alex, and Nora) went to South Africa to conduct training for civic leaders in what was still a volatile and dangerous place but was also a nation beginning to wrestle with the opportunities and challenges of political emancipation.

And one of my proudest accomplishments over

my forty-year career in organizing has been the fact that I found and helped train Dave Fleischer. Dave has gone on to become perhaps the premier organizer in the LBGTQ world. So I want to emphasize that I appreciate the value of individual rights and revere many of those who have fought to secure them. But at times, our society has tended toward an over-emphasis on individual rights and under-emphasis on institutional life, and that over-emphasis on individual rights and individual grievances has led to unintended and unhealthy consequences, such as those documented by DJ Jaffe in his book, *Insane Consequences*. Take the issue of mental health again. Nearly four decades ago, as the dreadful conditions in many asylums were being exposed, legal and advocacy groups sought to protect the rights of the mentally ill by making it impossible to impose treatment on them without their consent. The right to privacy was pushed to the limit—eventually denying even the most immediate family members of the mentally ill access to their drug regimens. For many people with milder forms of mental illness, this made some sense.

And there were certainly many times in the not-so-distant past when improper treatment was imposed either out of professional incompetence or by family members who did not have the best interests of those mentally ill at heart. But pushed to the extreme, this passion for individual privacy has condemned approximately 4% of those with serious mental illness into homelessness or imprisonment today.

So here we have the logical outcome for those suffering from mental illness and their loved ones from what William Sullivan described as the system of ideas championed by John Locke and Thomas Hobbes: the individual is conceived independently of social relationships, including immediate family relationships, with the ultimate value being an individual's will and preference, even if an individual with serious mental illness is often in no position to appreciate the consequences of his or her will or preference. "The concepts of philosophic liberalism," says Sullivan in his book, *Reconstructing Public Philosophy*, "were forged in polemic, as weapons for emancipating European social life from what early liberals regarded as the destructive and inequitable dominance of special privilege and monopoly in the regimes of early modern Europe. Liberal thought has never wholly lost this emancipatory edge, and from the seventeenth century to the present the defense of freedom for the individual has been its main theme."

And this is where both modern progressives and modern libertarians strike a common chord. For those on the right, these chords are struck when people call for local control, no new taxes, less government, fewer regulations, vouchers for housing or education, and more. For those on the left, the chords resonate when people insist on absolute privacy for the mentally ill, as well as other issues. Uncomfortable as libertarians and progressives are with each other, their positions on mental health are obviously not helping the mentally ill.

This tendency toward individual rights over institutional obligations also shows itself in the preference by progressives for movements and mobilizations rather than organizations and institutions. These loose gatherings of thousands or even tens of thousands, like the science march in Washington in April of 2017 (which I literally ran into as I headed out for a jog that day) highlight the weaknesses of protesting a single cause and focusing on a single opponent. Other than presence, such an event asks very little from the individuals involved. Literally anything goes, however: any sign, no matter how outrageous; any slogan, no matter how offensive; any image, no matter how grotesque. There was no clear accounting of turnout—of who brought how many followers and who failed to meet his or her goal. There is no institutional dues base for the movement—no consistent financial commitment discussed and agreed to by those participating. Funds for such events and movements are raised from outside donors or by passing the hat—either literally or electronically. And there is no system for keeping track of follow-up activities. Such mobilizations allow organizers and participants to have it both ways—to preserve their fundamental commitment to individual rights and their suspicion of all things institutional while participating in activities that give the impression of some level of organizational power. I would argue that that this impression is an illusion.

Here is another instance of synergy with the Internet and social media platforms. The Internet provides every individual, at all times and with almost no constraints or filters, with opportunities to express and augment individual preference and individual will. It is also the perfect medium for the simplification of inherently complex problems. Social media enable almost total individual freedom of expression. But that comes with a cost: the ceding of enormous power, the power to analyze and control, to monopolies like Amazon and Google and Facebook and Twitter and Microsoft. To young adults, who almost always consider social media to be great new tools, I say (at the risk of being called grumpy and behind the times): "Yes, but technology's actually a Trojan Horse. You let it in willingly. You celebrate it as a remarkable gift and celebrate your skill at using it. You promote it because you believe it makes your generation special and hip. But it comes loaded with dangers and threats you don't see or feel or admit. It is operated by monopolistic billionaires who sell your personal preferences and tendencies to commercial buyers and give your information to security agencies without so much as a single libertarian objection. In essence you are being used, mined, and played."

6

Why do we think individually
and not institutionally?

THE DISTRACTION
AND DETERIORATION
OF SO MANY
MEDIATING INSTITUTIONS

The sixth and last (and perhaps most important) factor in the decline of people's institutions is the distraction and deterioration of our many mediating institutions—religious, civic, labor, educational, political—over the past sixty-five years. I've spent many thousands of hours in parishes and congregations, in denominations and faith groups, and with union locals and their state affiliates that have all been caught in a long cycle of decline. Yes, demographics have changed. Families have moved. Communities that once were stable and filled with people who were Catholic, or Jewish, or United Methodist, or Lutheran have become more mixed and less attached to these local institutions. Yes, in the case of labor, there have been relentless attacks on unions—consistently from the private sector and the right side of the political spectrum but also from modern Democrats who embrace globalization and the ethos of Wall Street and Silicon Valley and distance themselves from organized workers.

There have been self-inflicted wounds as well. Many mediating institutions have become increasingly bureaucratic—filled with endless meetings and multiplying programs and position papers. Their original founding leaders, their original sense of mission, their original stories of trial and error are faded memories, replaced by cautious managers. Their ability and desire to relate, even to their own members, much less to people beyond their walls, have atrophied in many cases. Many of these institutions are stale and stuck and ripe for the taking by more focused and nimble opponents. Their collapse calls into question the whole notion of whether mediating institutions can be viable in the current context. And this gives those who think individually and operate individually an even greater sense of their own superiority and inevitable victory.

But a fearful synergy is not the same as inevitability. I believe that the formidable challenges facing our nation now, however daunting, are different in scale—but not in kind—to the crises threatening

New York City four decades ago. What can be done to address those challenges today?

Institutions are made, not born. And they are unmade—over time—by errant actions or failures to act, by internal trends or external pressures. All organizing, as we say in the IAF, is a process of dis-organizing or re-organizing institutions. Leaders of institutions can decide when and where they need to disorganize and how and where they would benefit from reorganizing. But if they don't disorganize and reorganize, other institutions and forces will drive this process from the outside or else a slow drift into decline will sap the institutional energy from within.

The robust and fully populated New York City of the 1940s and 1950s had undergone three decades of disorganization and little or no reorganization by the mid-1970s, when the city nearly went bust. So had the Ohio River valley towns of Portsmouth and Ironton, which in their heyday were shipping and transportation and manufacturing centers. So had the docks of Kearney, New Jersey, the steel mills of the southeast corner of Chicago, the lakefront cities of Indiana, and many hundreds of other cities, counties, and towns throughout the US.

In the language of John Kotter, a Harvard Business School writer's essay, "What Leaders Really Do," American institutions became over-managed and under-led. "Management is about coping with complexity. Its practices and procedures are largely a response to one of the most significant developments of the twentieth century: the emergence of large organizations.... Leadership, by contrast, is about coping with change.... Major changes are more and more necessary to survive and compete effectively in this new environment. More change always demands more leadership."

Kotter describes the main functions of *management* as: first, planning and budgeting; second, organizing and staffing; and third, controlling and problem solving. *Leadership*, Kotter says in contrast, sets a direction instead of planning and budgeting; aligns its membership, rather than its staff; and initiates action on specific, immediate, and winnable issues rather than trying to control and solve problems (which just postpones more radical responses, often half-baked, for someone else to come up with).

As the pace and scale of change kept increasing in the United States, as the need to cope with change grew, the nation's business schools and law schools kept minting more managers, not more leaders. In the 1970s, the responses of the New York elites—in both parties, on Wall Street, in the media, and on most points along the ideological spectrum—was *"benign neglect"* and *"planned shrinkage."* This was an attempt by *managers* to cope with an even more complex and troubled city. They created new programs, hired more staff, budgeted more for disconnected social services, tried to solve discrete problems. What they did not want to deal with was organized people and their institutions.

In the current crisis, these same elites on a national and international level are once again trying to manage, not lead. They are not setting new directions, aligning people and institutions in new ways, and motivating the leaders of those institutions. This is what needs to be done and what the IAF is attempting to do in about sixty cities in the US and a few places oversees.

But our kind of organizing—leaders trained and skilled in the art and science of both improving existing institutions and creating new institutions—is in very short supply. And no wonder. Beyond the IT and tech sectors—who in part value disruption and innovation but have also centralized profit and power and stifled new business starts in recent decades—there is no place, no school, hardly even a language for the kind of institutional reorganizing and new institutional creation needed now.

Here's a comparison that might sharpen this point. When we IAF organizers ask parents what they hope to see in a quality school for their children, we often hear two things: safety (secure doors, metal detectors, security personnel) and order (uniforms, quiet, obedience). Just for the record, we are for these kinds of things, with some limitations. But the reason that we hear very little other than those two themes is that *the parents we ask have never seen or been inside of a school of high quality, where great teaching and learn-*

ing take place. So we often arrange to take them to such schools—great schools in similar communities to theirs, that are teaching similar students to their children but with much better results. And once people see and hear what a great school looks and sounds like—its rhythms and images and dynamics—they can begin to imagine what *their* local school could and should aspire to.

Many Americans, perhaps most, are like these parents. They have been born and raised in areas where the institutions around them have been in decline, sometimes sharp decline, their entire lives. All that they have seen, at best, is a group of decent managers coping with a level of complexity that keeps increasing and thus defeating their best efforts. At worst, they have observed cynical managers who have given up and set their sights on their own retirement and pensions, or inept managers who flail away but sink all the faster, or corrupt managers who strip the copper out of the half-abandoned institutions they are supposed to serve.

This is the stark reality that younger Americans

face, and that makes it somewhere between difficult and impossible for them to imagine, much less to relate to, institutions. The vast majority of the institutions that young people experience are failed or failing—mainline religious congregations, unions, local civic associations, school boards and parent-teacher associations, veterans' groups, farm bureaus, political parties at the local or ward level, downtown or neighborhood businesses. They walk down the streets of their cities and suburbs and towns and see the outward signs of institutional decline. Their parents and grandparents tell stories of a past where institutions thrived, humming with loyalty and energy and sense of purpose, but they don't see it. Perhaps their grandparents even met at a church social or union hall meeting or dance; but the church no longer hosts socials, if the church exists at all; the union hall is boarded up and abandoned; the VFW hall is basically a tavern for a dwindling number of aging vets.

Recently I met with a pastor in mid-sized town in southern Ohio. He had lost his son to heroin and committed his ministry to creating a congregation that welcomed those addicted and recovering from addiction. At the end of the meeting, he looked at me and said, "You're a busy man, aren't you?" I said that I supposed I was but wondered why he asked. He said, "Well, then you won't be coming back. This is nowhere. Busy people don't come back to nowhere." I simply said that he had no way of knowing I had spent my working life in places that had been written off, that had been declared 'nowhere' by those who thought they knew better. I went back to that man a month later, trying to figure out, with him and others, how to organize in scattered towns and small cities that had been as written off, just as East Brooklyn and the South Bronx had been forty years before.

By the way, among the new institutions in his county that are "innovative" and "disruptive" are the pill mills run by entrepreneurial doctors from Chicago or Detroit or somewhere else who prescribe a veritable river of opioids to the residents of a vast region once called "middle America." These contemporary white-collar criminals lead people inexorably to the heroin and other street dealers who use aggressive marketing techniques and high-tech sophisticated sales and distribution strategies to ensnare those who need a greater (and often cheaper) high than the one pushed on them by the billionaire producers of prescription drugs.

Not all new institutions young people experience are destructive. But several that are growing and expanding have distanced themselves from the larger public arena. The thousands of remarkable recovery groups created in reaction to the explosion in addiction are, by definition, designed to operate apart from the public, and they encourage participants to remain anonymous so that a free and frank exchange can occur. The vibrant evangelical congregations that have expanded rapidly in the past forty years have set a clear direction, but that direction is largely inward and individualistic. Unlike the institutions of the past, these newer institutions help people recover from the damage done in the larger world, but they don't equip and enable them to embark on a new and exciting direction, to align with people whom they respect and trust, to find motivation and stimulation in collective action. Many new institutions are a haven or refuge from the world, not a vehicle of economic or social mobility and progress.

In short, many young Americans are like those parents in an inner-city neighborhood who have never seen or experienced a quality school. And like those parents, deprived of memories or examples of vibrant people's institutions, they have an understandable default response to the question of what they hope the future will bring: they want less violence and crime and more safety and security; they want less chaos and uncertainty and more order and predictability. But they cannot imagine that they and their moribund institutions could ever have enough power to make those things happen. If anything, they tend to respond to political leaders (from Obama to Trump) who promise to deliver those outcomes but seldom if ever do.

CONCLUSION

Now that I'm sixty-eight years old and have been working as a professional organizer for four decades, people often ask me, with a bit of sorrow in their voices, how I feel about the state of the world. Their expectation, most of the time, is that I will add my own dose of sorrow to theirs. But that's not what I feel and not what I say. On the ground, in places like East Brooklyn or San Antonio and sixty or so other cities or counties in the country, I am part of a non-partisan political organizing culture that is engaged in meaningful work on a wide range of issues. Over those four decades, our organizations have re-ignited the living wage movement in the United States, beginning in Baltimore in 1994 and New York in 1996 and Texas in 2000 and beyond. We have done what people said could not be done by rebuilding devastated and neglected neighborhoods with housing affordable to the people who already lived in those areas—what we call "revitalization without gentrification." We have pioneered the earliest health care innovations in Illinois in 1999 and Massachusetts in 2006, which brought access and affordable care to young adults and poor and working-class families. We launched a new kind of public school—smaller in scale, locally supported, begun from scratch, created around a theme—before the charter public schools ever arrived. This list goes on and on and is expanding and deepening as I write.

Recently, during the month of October 2017, more than 1000 citizens met with the mayoral candidates in Jersey City to focus on the development of 200 vacant acres there. The next night 300 citizens from across New York City met in a synagogue on the East Side with three pioneers in the effort to divert those with mental illness from jail or prison—Judge Stephen Leifman from Miami Dade-County, Leon

Evans from San Antonio, and Judge Matthew D'Emic from Brooklyn. The next day, our New York organizations sponsored a conference with 125 professional in these fields. Six days later, our Brooklyn and other New York City affiliates staged a massive rally of 6,000 citizens, in the rain, outside of City Hall, calling on the self-described "progressive" mayor of New York to deliver truly affordable housing throughout the city. Alexis de Tocqueville himself would not have been disappointed by these examples of voluntary leaders, connected to local associations and congregations, taking pragmatic aim at difficult issues that our "managers" in government and the private sector have largely given up on or decided to ignore.

These citizen actions—and scores more like them around the country—are the outward signs of a robust civic culture that continues to thrive. Like sports, the practice of that culture is simple but hard. It depends on an understanding of the radical power of public relationships—the kinds of relationships that still can only be initiated and built through face-to-face, one-to-one engagement. It depends on applying the challenge that George Orwell succinctly described this way: "To see what is in front of one's nose needs a constant struggle." We translate Orwell's insight into a habit of understanding power—who has it, how it operates, what impact it creates, how to build it, how to wield it effectively. It implies the rejection of stereotypes, assumptions, projections, or prepackaged ideologies—all used as substitutes when people cannot get close enough to reality to see what is in front of their noses.

Understanding power and wielding power in this way enables citizens to avoid the traps that ensnare so many—one being apathy, a life of detached spectatorship; another being what one academic calls "political hobbyism," casually dipping in and out of the public arena when time or attention span permit; a third being an obsession with unilateral power— power divorced from relationships and values, the power to dominate, the power to force others to conform or be crushed.

The whole goal of creating an independent, nonpartisan, institutionally-based citizens organization can be summarized this way: it is a vehicle that enables decent, normal, passionate, people to observe power dynamics, to make their own informed judgements about them, and to relate reciprocally and with mutual respect to one another across any divisions that might exist between them.

Once these public relationships have been built and the power analysis done, it's important for these organized citizens to act together and then to evaluate those actions. Those evaluations are another form of the ongoing training and development of leaders that we in the IAF insist upon throughout this entire process.

So, I live and work in a world where this kind of organizing is happening on a daily basis. It is not perfect. It is not always successful. It has its own challenges and stresses. But it is healthy, exciting, and even joyful at times. And it resonates with some of the very oldest and best features of the American experiment

It is unfortunate, and one of my regrets, that many Americans, perhaps most Americans, do not have an opportunity to engage in this kind of public life and public action. Lacking this kind of civic antidote, they are exposed to the dynamics that take place in Washington, in the mainstream and alternative media, and, increasingly, in social media. They never get close enough to see what is in front of their noses. They never negotiate directly with major power figures from other sectors and instead rely on second- and third-hand interpretations, often colored by ideological leanings, that are fed to them. They repeat outdated tactics—tweeting, texting, signing a online petitions, occasionally going to a haphazardly organized protest—and then retreat when the tactics fail to generate a useful reaction or create a constructive result.

The challenge that we face today—nearly eighty years after modern citizens' organizing began to take root in the US—is three-fold.

The first is how to nurture a culture of relationship building, power analysis, leadership training, and effective action so that it becomes a felt reality in a much broader set of communities and constituencies. No new political savior and neither political party can create this culture. Only local citizens can.

The second challenge is to create more critical masses of constructive change—in the field of criminal justice and mental health, in the arena of city and regional rebuilding, in the world of safe and affordable public transportation and housing, and in other areas that generate the kind of constructive chain reactions I have seen in Brooklyn and other cities and counties. Those who have already succeeded—and I have mentioned several examples here—need to boast about it a bit more. Those who are still struggling to achieve results need to see that their local efforts have implications for hundreds of other communities across the country.

Third, we need to add a new challenge to the formidable list of issues we have already addressed: that is, how to generate new long-term work that pays American families a living wage. A leader in an area decimated by opioids told me, "My daughter is in recovery, which we are thankful for. But now what? There are no jobs here. Does she just sit home and look out the window?" I have some ideas about how to do this, but those ideas belong in another essay.

Like so many others, I'm haunted by the "deaths of despair" that Professors Deaton and Case described in their ground-breaking studies and by the stories I've observed, read about, and heard over and over again during my long career in organizing. I'm convinced that this death toll will continue to mount if our nation does not generate millions of jobs accessible to what once was called the "working" class. I believe the emergence of a new era of living wage work—itself the product of a robust and revitalized civic culture—can stop the upward rise of the terrible trend lines I referred to at the start of this book. Those lines will level off and begin to fall only when American families and communities see that they can once again live lives of promise and opportunity. And those living lives of promise and opportunity must have the energy and optimism to rescue struggling institutions and create new institutions that will reinforce the foundation for our Republic going forward.

SELECTED BIBLIOGRAPHY ON
THE DECLINE OF PEOPLE'S INSTITUTIONS

Bowling Alone: The Collapse and Revival of American Community, Robert Putnam

Buying Time: The Delayed Crisis of Democratic Capitalism, Second Edition, Wofgang Streeck

Caught in the Middle: America's Heartland in the Age of Globalism, Richard Longworth

Crazy: A Father's Search Through America's Mental Health Madness, Pete Earley

Dreamland: The True Tale of America's Opiate Epidemic, Sam Quinones

Glass House: The 1% Economy and the Shattering of the All-American Town, Brian Alexander

Insane Consequences: How the Mental Health Industry Fails the Mentally Ill, DJ Jaffee

Listen, Liberal: Or, What Ever Happened to the Party of the People, Thomas Frank

Makers and Takers: The Rise of Finance and the Fall of American Business, Rana Foroohar

PEOPLE'S INSTITUTIONS IN DECLINE

Mortality and Morbidity in the 21st Century, Anne Case and Angus Deaton, the Brookings Institution

Move Fast and Break Things: How Facebook, Google, and Amazon Cornered Culture and Undermined, Jonathan Taplin

Political Hobbyism: A Theory of Mass Behavior, Eitan Hersh

Strangers in Their Own Land: Anger and Mourning on the American Right, Arlie Russell Hochschild

The Third Coast: When Chicago Built the American Dream, Thomas Dyja

The Unwinding: An Inner History of the New America, George Packer

When I Was a Child, I Read Books, Marilynne Robinson

REFLECTING WITH SCRIPTURE ON COMMUNITY ORGANIZING

by Rev. Jeff Krehbiel

The former pastor of the Church of the Pilgrims in Washington, D.C., and co-chair of the Washington Interfaith Network offers reflections on four passages from Scripture and how they relate to the experience of community organizing. He also offers a Group Study Guide for congregational use. 60 pages, paperback

EFFECTIVE ORGANIZING FOR CONGREGATIONAL RENEWAL

by Michael Gecan

The author of *Going Public* and co-executive director of the Industrial Areas Foundation describes how the tools of organizing can and are transforming Protestant, Catholic, Jewish and Muslim congregations. Included are five case studies of congregations that have used this process to grow. 54 pages, paperback

REBUILDING OUR INSTITUTIONS

by Ernesto Cortes, Jr.

Ernie Cortes, the co-executive director of the Industrial Areas Foundation, argues that community organizing cultivates the practices needed for democracy to thrive, including one-on-one relational meetings, house meetings, and systematic reflection on them afterwards. This book contains several examples from organizations in California, Louisiana, and Texas that helped local congregations and other mediating institutions identify, confront, and change things that were destroying their families and communities. 30 pages, paperback